COOKING WITH A HALOGEN OVEN:
The Only Halogen Oven Cookbook You Will Ever Need

P. Karn

Table of Contents

Introduction

Congratulations on getting your new Halogen oven! I know you must be very excited and have fallen in love with it so much that you don't even want to use it just yet. Well, one day you are going to need to use it in order to make a wonderful meal for your family and this is where this book comes in to help you through that process.

Are you the type of person who is trying to live a healthier lifestyle? Are you the person who simply wants to be a master chef in your own home? Whatever the case may be in this eBook you will find an array of different delicious dishes that you can choose from to satisfy any taste bud in your home and you can do it without breaking a sweat.

Now that you have your Halogen oven you need to keep in mind that the better you take care of it, the longer it will last. In this eBook besides coming across delicious recipes, you will also find a variety of helpful tips on what is the best way to care for your Halogen oven and what kind of benefits you will experience now that you have your oven.

Chapter One: Now That You Have Your Halogen Oven, What Exactly Is It?

Before you can even begin cooking with your new halogen oven, I highly recommend that you read the instructions and safety information that came along with it in the box. These will have helpful and useful information, which you can use for future use and that I guarantee you will not regret later.

One of the main questions that you may find that you are asking yourself is what in the world have I bought with the well earned cash I recently made? While your oven make look the same as other ovens on the market today and they pretty much work in the same way, your own oven will be unique simply because it is your own.

One of the many things that nearly every single oven has in common with another is that they come with the same basic parts. These parts include:

1. 2 cooking racks (1 for the lower part of the oven and 1 for the higher part of the oven).
2. 1 pair of cooking tongs.
3. A top lid, which is used to cover up the inner part of your halogen oven.
4. A timer knob upon the actual halogen oven.
5. A knob used to control the temperature of your oven.
6. A safety switch.
7. A glass bowl.

You should know that you can easily purchase other special parts for your oven such as an extender rings which can be used to cook larger foods such as a whole chicken by going either on to eBay or Amazon and conducting a simple search for the parts you are looking for.

How Does Your Halogen Oven Work?

If you are not sure how to use your halogen oven, don't worry. You will soon be able to figure it out how to use it for yourself in no time at all. All that you need to do is turn your halogen oven. Once you do that the infrared waves that your oven produces will begin to warm up your oven by sending around the main bowl as fast as possible. There is also a fan located at the top of your oven that will help increase the speed of which your oven becomes hot.

This is when you will be using the temperature control knob upon your halogen oven to set the temperature to what you are looking for. The one thing you will notice here is that your oven can reach such a high temperature that it can easily surpass the average temperature of a conventional oven. Once you have the temperature set you are ready to cook up your first savory meal.

What Are The Cooking Benefits Of Your Halogen Oven

There are many cooking benefits that you will experience when using your new halogen oven. For starters you will be able to not only bake your food, but you will be able to slow cook, steam, grill and defrost your food as well. Another benefit to using your halogen oven for cooking purposes is that this oven has the ability to clean itself, which will save you on cleaning time in the long run.

A halogen oven is also portable as long as you have an outlet to plug it in you have the potential to bring it anywhere such as in your RV if you are driving around the country or on business trips where the hotel room you are staying in does not have an oven where you can cook your meals.

Other cooking benefits to using your Halogen oven are that there is no need for you to worry about bending down to retrieve heavy pans of food from your stove as your oven can be placed upon any sturdy countertop, it will regulate temperature inside the oven automatically so you never have to worry about your food burning and your food comes out much more juicy and succulent than cooking in any traditional oven.

Chapter Two: The Health Benefits, Advantages and Disadvantages of Your Halogen Oven

In the last chapter we discussed the variety of different reasons as to what kind of cooking benefits you will experience with your new Halogen oven. However, you may be surprised to discover that you will experience a variety of healthy benefits to using your oven for your cooking needs as well. Surprisingly using a halogen oven is a much healthier alternative to cooking your food than using a conventional oven.

To start, when you are using your halogen oven there is no need to use butter or oil to help whatever meat you are cooking to become juicy upon completion. Because these ovens heat up very quickly, this gives poultry and meat the opportunity to heat up quickly as well and to cook literally in its own juices. Keep in mind, just because you are not using butter or oil does not mean that your meat will come out bland. It will come out tasting as if it was cooked in a professional restaurant.

Are you the type of person who needs to constantly trim the fat on their poultry or meat in order to have a healthier meal? With your new halogen oven there is no need to worry about that any more. When you cook the meat in your oven the excess fat will drip off of it and you can collect it in a tray to dispose of after you are finished cooking.

Another health benefit to cooking your meals in a halogen oven is that you don't have to wait long for your meals to cook. Why is this considered a health benefit? Well, let's say that you are on a diet and you need to eat your dinner by a certain time each and every day. If you are running slightly behind on schedule you don't need to worry as your food will be able to cook much faster than it would in any kind of traditional oven. For example, if you were craving a thick piece of steak it would only take 10-15 minutes to cook in your halogen oven. If you are on a strict time schedule, using a Halogen oven is something that can help get you back on the right course.

The Advantages of Your Halogen Oven

As you probably have guessed, your Halogen oven has come with an array of different advantages that you will have the chance to see firsthand. One of the many advantages this oven has is that there is no need to spend hours scrubbing away at it in order to clean it. Luckily for you this oven comes with a handy self-cleaning function that cleans the oven for you so you can spend the time relaxing and enjoying yourself then straining yourself in order to clean it.

Another advantage to using this oven is that you save endless time on cooking then you would in a traditional oven. Remember, food is able to cook in a matter of seconds in this kind of oven than it would in a traditional oven. This is what makes the entire cooking process easier on you in the long run. This also give you the chance to relax knowing that your food will be completely cooked through so you don't have to stand vigilant near the oven thinking that you are about to burn your meal. It is no wonder that this oven has become increasingly popular over the past couple of years.

The Disadvantages of Your Halogen Oven

As with everything, this oven isn't without its own set of disadvantages. One of the main disadvantages to using this oven is that since it is a brand new appliance in your home, you may not know how to use it right away. Of course these kinds of things take time to learn and the more you use it, the easier it will be to use it in the future. Make sure that you take the time to practice using it so you do not make any mistake the first time you prepare a meal in it.

How To Care For Your Halogen Oven

Taking care of your Halogen oven is relatively easy, as long as you do it correctly the very first time. To clean it by hand, there are a few things that you will need to do in a specific order so that you can clean it properly and safely.

1. Make sure that you unplug your oven first. This will give it time to cool down to a safe temperature that you will be able to touch the inside of it without burning yourself in the process.

2. Once the glass bowl of your oven cools down completely, you can clean all of the parts there with warm soapy water. Or if you have a dishwasher you can safely wash it in there as these parts are all dishwasher safe.

3. In order to clean the fan cover that comes with your oven, you will need to remove the screw first before you can take the cover completely off. Wash the cover in warm soapy water and make sure that it dries completely before you re-assemble it.

The Self-Cleaning Function

Your new halogen oven comes with an amazing self-cleaning option that is perfect for you if you do not want to spend time cleaning it yourself. If you want to use the self-cleaning "wash" control simply follow these steps.

1. Make sure that you remove any excess food that has been left in the bowl and make sure that any excess fat is removed.

2. Add a half of an inch of warm water into the glass bowl and add a drop or two of dishwashing liquid as well. Make sure that you put the glass lid back on and then turn the control knob to the "wash" setting.

3. Set the timer control to 10-15 minutes. The time you will set will ultimately depend on how dirty your glass bowl is.

4. If you want to clean the cooking rack as well you can put them inside the glass bowl. Once you set the timer the bowl and the cooking racks will clean themselves in a time efficient manner.

5. Once the oven has finished cleaning, wait for it to cool down before you remove any parts. Sometimes you may need to finish off the cleaning by scrubbing away at any dirt spots that had failed to be cleaned during the "wash" stage.

Storing Your Halogen Oven

Just like cleaning, storing your halogen oven is just as important in order to care for it properly. The best way to store the oven is to make sure that the oven has cooled completely before you attempt to store it as this will reduce the risk of your hurting yourself. Place your halogen oven in a cool and dry place within your home and cover it up so dust particles do not get inside the glass bowl.

Delicious Main Entrée Recipes

Delicious Roast Beef with A Side of Horseradish

If you are looking for a great recipe to please the members of your family, this is definitely the dish for you. Roast Beef can be served with a variety of sides such as a yummy Yorkshire pudding, a bowl of steamed vegetables, a side of roasted garlic potatoes or maybe a bowl of delicious mashed potatoes with homemade gravy.

The exact timing for this kind of recipe with vary due to a variety of different factors such as how big of a cut you are using, the size of the meat you plan to use or what your personal taste is. Make sure to cut away at the roast beef every couple of minutes to check how pink the inside is and stop cooking once the beef has reached the color you want.

Serving Size: 4 to 6

Ingredients:
- 1 Beef Joint
- A Pinch of Black Pepper

- 300 Ml of Red Wine
- 2 Tbsp. of Golden Syrup
- 4 Tbsp. of Horseradish
- 2 Tbsp. of Brown Sugar

Directions

1. Preheat your oven to 410 degrees. You can do this two different ways such as using the preheating setting or you can manually set the temperature.

2. Using a medium size mixing bowl, add the horseradish, brown sugar and golden syrup. Combine them until well blended and add the pinch of Black Pepper for taste.

3. Place the beef that you purchased in a roasting pan and then place it on the lower rack of your Halogen oven. Cook for approximately 20 minutes. Then turn down the temperature at the 20 minute mark to 350 degrees Fahrenheit.

4. Once you set the temperature down, coat the meat well with you horseradish concoction and continuing cooking for another 20 minutes for every pound of meat that you have. To prevent the meat from darkening until it resembles burnt meat, I suggest that you cover it with a thin layer of tin foil.

5. Halfway through cooking you will want to add your red wine. The red wine will mix thoroughly with the meat juices and these two can even be used to make a beef gravy stock.

6. Once the roast beef is fully cooked, turn off your halogen oven. You will need to wrap the meat in tin foil and let it sit

for 20 minutes. While it cools you can use this time to prepare a natural gravy to go along with the roast beef.

Roast Beef Gravy

1. 1 tsp. of Corn flour-mix it in with a little bit of beef stock and pour it into the dish that hold the natural juices from the roast beef and the red wine. Heat it up very gently and stir until it thickens. Serve and enjoy.

6. Once your beef has been fully cooked, wrap it securely in a layer of tin foil and leave it to cool for at least 20 minutes. While it cools prepare to make your homemade gravy. To do this mix both 1 tsp. of Corn Flour and ¼ cup of beef stock and add it to your roasting pan. You will want to heat it gently and stir it constantly until the gravy thickens. Serve your roast beef with either a side of fresh vegetables or a couple of roasted potatoes.

Mexican Quesadillas

Now, quesadillas are one of the most savory dishes you can make and the best part is you can either make them as an entrée or as an appetizer. Originally from the country of Mexico, these yummy snacks have made their way into the United States where it continues to thrive and satisfy even the pickiest of eaters. Usually I like to fill my own quesadillas up like a large sandwich, packing it with as much chicken, cheese, steak or some other filling as much as possible. Feel free to use your own ingredients and to stuff your own quesadilla as much as you like.

This recipe is one of the most basic kinds of quesadillas that you can make and include such ingredients as cheese, onion, tomato and chili.

Servings: 1-2

Ingredients:
- 2 Flour Tortillas

- 1-2 Tomatoes sliced up (all depending on your own taste)
- 1 White Onion, sliced
- Sharp Cheddar Cheese, shredded
- Chili, sliced to your own taste
- Dash of Salt and Pepper

Directions

1. Using a greased baking tray, place one floured tortilla upon it.

2. On top of the flour tortilla sprinkle whatever fillings you have chosen. Next you will need to season the quesadilla to your own personal taste.

3. Place the second flour tortilla on top and make sure that you press down upon it firmly.

4. Place the tray on the high rack. Next set the temperature to 410 degrees Fahrenheit and cook the quesadilla for only 5 to 8. You will need to cook the quesadilla until it is golden brown and the cheese begins to melt.

5. Take out your quesadilla and cut into large wedges. Serve with Guacamole, Sour Cream and Salsa and enjoy.

Yummy Garlic Butter Baked Prawns

This incredibly simply dish will surely impress your friends and family. If you have never had prawns before I can assure you that you will become quickly addicted to this recipe.

Ingredients:

- 1 Tbsp. Olive Oil
- 1 Stick of Butter
- Lemon Juice
- 3-4 Cloves of Garlic, Minced
- 1 Handful of Fresh Parsley, chopped finely
- 1 ½ lbs of Prawns
- Dash of Salt and Pepper
- A Handful of Parsley To Be Used For Garnish

Servings:4

Total Cooking Time:12 Minutes

Total Preparation Time: 5-10 Minutes

Directions

1. Place both the olive oil and butter in a bowl that is oven proof. Next add your garlic.

2. Place a rack onto the lowest place possible and set the temperature of your oven at 480 degrees Fahrenheit. As soon as the butter begins to melt, remove it from the halogen oven immediately.

3. Once it is removed from heat stir in your lemon zest, lemon juice and your finely chopped parsley. Next add a dash of pepper to your own liking.

4. Next you will want to add your prawns to the dish with your stirred butter mixture. Toss it gently to make sure that all of the prawns are coated nicely with the mixture.

5. Cover your dish with a lid or if you would prefer you can use two sheets of tin foil to cover it. Place your dish back into your halogen oven and set the temperature to 375 degrees Fahrenheit. Cook your prawns for 10 minutes or until they are cooked to your own personal taste.

6. Remove from the oven and serve with parsley as garnish. Enjoy!

Pork Chops Served With Steamed Courgette

I am a huge fan of freshly cooked pork chops and I know that I am not the only one. This recipe makes one of the most succulent and moist pork chops you will ever taste. This dish is great for a lazy Sunday night dinner or for pleasing your entire family at a family reunion. When following this recipe keep in mind that you may need to cook the pork chops for a few extra minutes but this will all depend on the overall thickness of the meat itself.

Cooking Time: About 30 Minutes

Ingredients:
- 4 Pork Chops
- 2-3 Courgettes (get as many as will fit comfortably in your Halogen Oven)
- A Bit of Oil
- Garlic, chopped (use according to taste)
- Dash of Salt and Pepper
- Dash of Parsley and Cilantro

- ½ tsp of Tarragon
- ½ tsp of Ground Coriander Seed
- 1 Sheet of Tin Foil

Directions

1. Preheat your halogen oven to 200 degrees Fahrenheit and make sure that you place both a low rack and high rack into your bowl to ensure the pork chops can cook evenly.

2. Wash the Courgettes and slice them thinly. Place a couple of slices in a sheet of tin foil and add your oil, salt, pepper and garlic.

3. Cover the Courgettes completely and place upon the highest rack. You will need to cook these for 5-6 minutes depending on your personal taste.

4. After 5-6 minutes move the covered Courgettes on the lowest rack in your bowl and begin preparing the pork chops for cooking.

5. Wash the pork chops and then pat them dry. Once they are dry season both sides of the chops with some pepper, salt, cilantro, parsley, ground Coriander seed and Tarragon.

6. Place the newly seasoned pork chops upon the highest rack inside your bowl and cook them for 12-17 minutes. The cooking time will all depend on the overall thickness of the pork chops that you buy.

7. Remove the Courgettes and Pork Chops From Heat. Once cooled to an ideal temperature serve them with veggies or mashed potatoes and enjoy.

Succulent Baked Potato With Savory Roast Chicken

A baked potato, also known as a jacket potato pretty much can go with any dish. However, the best dish that it can be paired with is a savory roast chicken that will be sure to please even the pickiest of eaters. Using the right amount of herbs and the right kind of cheese for your potato will leave the people you cook for begging for seconds.

Ingredients:

- 1 Large Baking Potato
- Raw Pieces of Chicken, defrosted

Directions

1. Place a low rack into your halogen oven dish and preheat the oven to 220 degrees Fahrenheit.

2. Make sure that you wash the potato thoroughly and prick it with a fork multiple times all over its surface. Next you will want to rub the potato with either a little bit of oil or butter depending on your taste.

3. Cook the potato at 220 degrees for about 30 minutes. Of course the cooking time will vary depending on the actual size of the potato. If you are not sure if the potato is soft enough you can easily check it every 10 minutes or so.

4. Next wash the raw pieces of chicken and then pat them dry. Place the chicken next to the potato once the potato has reach ideal softness.

5. You will want to cook the chicken for a total of 20 minutes. Cook on one side for 10 minutes and then the other side for another 10.

6. I would recommend serving this dish with a freshly made salad and enjoy.

Yummy Vegetarian Cheese and Herb Soufflés

If there is one dish that seems to be every household chefs nightmare, it is the soufflé. They are one of the many dishes that are not that easy to make, but they are the ones that happen to be the most impressive. The truth is just looking at a picture of a soufflé is intimidating and makes us fear it. However, this kind of recipe can be very straightforward as long as you allow it to be so. The first time you make it you may have some difficulty but I can tell you this from experience: the more you practice, the easier it is to make and the more often you can impress any guests that you may be having over for dinner.

Serving Size:2

Ingredients:

- ¼ of a lb. of Butter
- ¼ cup of Flour
- 1/3 cup Milk
- ½ cup of Ricotta Cheese

- ¼ cup of Parmesan Cheese, Grated
- 2 Eggs
- 1 egg white
- Dash of Parsley, Oregano, Chives and Thyme

Directions:

1. Before you can even begin to make your soufflés, you will first need to make a basic white sauce, which all soufflés contain. To do this you will melt butter in a separate pan then add in the flour slowly. Stir with a large wooden spoon and stir enough that there are no lumps left in the mixture. Next add the milk and switch to using a whisk. Cook the sauce until it thickens and lastly remove it from heat.

2. You will need to add both the Parmesan and ricotta cheese. Then add 2 egg yolks and the herbs you will be using for seasoning.

3. Using a clean bowl add 3 egg whites. Beat the whites until you are able to form stiff peaks from the mixture. Once this happens you will need to fold your cheese mixture into the egg whites.

4. Grease your individual soufflé dishes and pour in your new mixture until it reaches the top of the dishes.

5. You will then need to preheat your halogen oven to 350 degrees Fahrenheit. Once preheated place your soufflé dishes into the oven. You will need to first put them in a tray containing water so that the water reaches the middle of the soufflé dishes. Place the soufflé dishes on the medium rack.

6. Cook your soufflés for at least 20-25 minutes or until they are golden brown.

7. Remove from heat and make sure to serve them immediately.

Delicious Feta and Spinach Pie

This dish is a great choice for vegetarians or anybody who wishes to be on a healthier diet. You have the option of serving this dish with a bowl of fresh mixed veggies or perhaps even a salad.

Serving Size:4-6

Ingredients:

- ¼ cup of Butter
- 6 Sheets of Filo Pastry
- 1 ½ cups of Baby Spinach Leaves, tear them roughly
- 1 cup of Feta Cheese, crumbled
- Salt and Pepper for seasoning
- Λ pinch of Sesame Seeds

Directions

1. Preheat your Halogen oven to 380 degrees Fahrenheit.

2. Melt the ¼ cup of butter in a separate saucepan and place it into your Halogen oven bowl. Keep a careful eye on it to ensure that it doesn't burn.

3. In a pie dish add 3 layers of the pastry sheets. While you place them make sure that you rub butter between every layer. All of pastry sheets to hang over the edges of your pie dish.

4. Next you will need to place a thin layer of spinach leaves and then a thin layer of the crumbled feta cheese. Season it slightly with salt and pepper to taste. Repeat until all ingredients have been used.

5. Add 3 more layers of pastry sheet on top of the filling and brush butter in between each layer. Next you will want to bring the edges of the pastry sheet together to form a crust and to remove any excess pastry sheet.

6. Brush your finished pastry with butter and sprinkle a dash of sesame seeds on top of it.

7. Place your pastry on the lowest rack of your halogen oven and bake for 30 to 40 minutes or until a golden brown color.

8. Serve and enjoy.

Juicy Roast Chicken

Are you the kind of person who has always wanted to make a whole roast chicken but didn't know how to do it? This recipe makes cooking a whole chicken a simple process and you have the option of adding your own ingredients to it to make it your own unique recipe.

Ingredients:

- 1 Large Chicken
- 2 Tbsp. of Sea Salt
- 1 Tsp. of Mixed Herbs
- 1 Tsp. of Black Pepper
- 2 Tbsp. of Olive Oil

Directions:

1. Wash the entire chicken thoroughly and pat it dry with a towel or napkin. Place your chicken directly onto the lower rack of your halogen oven.

2. In a separate bowl mix your olive oil, pepper, salt, mixed herbs and while using a pastry brush spread mixture over the entire bird.

3. Roast your chicken in the Halogen oven at 375 degrees Fahrenheit for 60 minutes or until the chicken is a crisp golden brown. To check if the chicken is done skewer the leg and if the juices comes out clear, it is done. If the juices are a slight pink, cook the chicken for an additional 10 minutes.

4. Serve with potatoes or a salad and enjoy.

Healthy Roasted Vegetables

For those who are living a healthier lifestyle or who wish to eat something a little healthier, this is the best recipe for you. You can use this recipe to mix with other halogen oven recipes such as roast beef or chicken or you can serve it all by itself.

Ingredients:

- 4 small potatoes, skin scrubbed and unpeeled
- 1 Green Pepper, thinly sliced
- 1 Yellow Pepper, thinly sliced
- 1 Orange Pepper, thinly sliced
- 2 white onions, sliced and quartered
- 10 cloves of Garlic, crushed
- 12 Cherry Tomatoes, thinly sliced
- 1 Courgette, sliced thinly
- 1 tsp. of Mixed Herbs including Parsley and fresh Basil
- A Dash of sea salt
- A Dash of Pepper

36

Directions:

1. Place all of the above ingredients in a large roasting dish. Toss these ingredients with olive oil, sprinkle with mixed herbs and season it to your taste.

2. Place the vegetables into your Halogen oven and place onto the lowest rack. Cook at 410 degrees Fahrenheit for 25 minutes. Remove from oven and set aside to cool slightly. Serve and enjoy.

Beef Casserole

This delicious and juicy stew is great for those who are feeling a bit under the weather in your home or for days that you just want to make a simple meal. This delicious stew can be served alongside a bowl of yummy vegetables or can be served with a few slices of bread.

Serving Size: About 4

Total Cooking and Preparation Time: 1 hour and 45 minutes

Ingredients

- 1.65 lbs. of Cubed Beef
- 1 Tbsp. of Oil
- 2 Tbsp. of Flour
- 1 Large White Onion of 4 Shallots, finely sliced
- 2 Large Carrots, sliced into small pieces
- ½ cup of Beef Stock
- ½ cup of Red Wine
- Dash of Salt and Pepper to Taste
- 1 tsp. of Cornflour

Directions:

1. Preheat your halogen oven to 350 degrees Fahrenheit.

2. While your oven is heating up using a large frying pan place your 1 Tbsp. of Oil and set it to heat.

3. While that is heating up roll the chunk of meat you will be using in a bowl of flour until coated well.

4. Being careful place the floured meat into the frying pan and sear them quickly. Searing will help to keep the beef juicy and the flour that you use will help to ensure that the stew is nice and thick upon completion.

5. Next you will want to place the carrots and the onion into a casserole dish with the meat that you seared.

6. Pour your beef stock and red on top of the carrots, onions and meat and season with a dash of salt and pepper to taste.

7. Place the casserole dish into your oven and cook for approximately 1 hour and 45 minutes.

Don't Forget To Thicken Your Stew

- Once your stew has completely finished cooking you will need to add 1 tsp. of corn flour and a little bit of cold water into your dish and mix it well.
- Serve and enjoy.

Stuffed Chicken Breasts with Creamy Butter Sauce

This is one delicious recipe that is not only simple to make, but it is one that the entire family can enjoy. This recipe incorporate many lovely flavors and with the use of ricotta cheese and ripened sweet tomatoes this recipe perfectly combines the right ingredients that help the chicken cook to near perfection and to cook in its juices, making it one of the juiciest pieces of chicken you will ever have.

Serving Size: Approximately 4

Total Cooking and Preparation Time: 50 minutes

Ingredients:

- ¼ cup of Sun Dried Tomatoes, Chopped
- 1 Tbsp. of Fresh Rosemary, Finely Chopped
- 1 tsp. of Fresh Thyme, Finely Chopped
- 4 Skinless and Boneless Chicken Breasts
- 4 Tbsp. of Ricotta Cheese
- 4 Thin Slices of Prosciutto Ham

Directions:

1. Preheat your Halogen oven to 375 degrees.

2. Using a separate bowl thoroughly mix your rosemary, thyme, sun dried tomatoes and ricotta cheese together until thoroughly combined.

3. Using a sharp knife cut slices into your chicken breasts and fill these slices with your cheese mixture.

4. Place your chicken into the halogen bowl and cook for 25-30 minutes. To check if you chicken is done pierce the hides with a knife and if the juices run clear then your chicken is fully cooked.

5. Remove your chicken and place the juices that are left over into a separate saucepan.

6. Next add a small amount of butter to your juices and mix until butter is fully combined. Pour over chicken and serve with a side of potatoes or mixed vegetables. Enjoy.

Tuna and Tomato Pasta

This recipe is a delicious dish that every member of your family will love regardless if they are an adult or a child. It is great tasting and ridiculously easy to make, making cleanup a cinch for you. It is also a great recipe to use to help your kids to cook their own meal for the first time, making a wonderful bonding experience for the entire family.

Serving Size: Approximately 2
Total Cooking and Preparation Time: 30 minutes

Ingredients:

- ½-1 cup of pasta (any kind that you like will be fine)
- 1 Small Onion, Chopped Finely
- 2 Tbsp. of Butter
- 1 Can of Tuna
- 1 Can of Italian Passata Tomatoes
- ½ cup of Parmesan Cheese

- Fresh Basil Leaves

Directions:

1. In a pan of boiling water with a touch of salt and olive oil added, cook your pasta over medium heat for about 12 to 15 minutes or until the pasta is al dente.

2. Once done drain the pasta and begin to make the sauce. Chop the onions and sauté them in a small frying pan with some butter and cook until the onions are soft and translucent. Add the pasta and heat for the next 2 minutes.

3. Drain your tuna and add to your pasta.

4. In a small baking pan add your pasta mixture and sprinkle the top with parmesan cheese. Bake the pasta at 400 degrees for 15 minutes or until the top is a nice golden brown color.

5. Add a few fresh basil leaves to garnish. Serve and enjoy.

Great Tasting Shepherd's Pie

This is the perfect dish to make all year round or whenever you want to impress your friends and family. Great to serve at dinner parties or just for a lazy Sunday dinner, this recipe is a luxurious version of Shepherd's Pie that you are most likely used to having.

Serving Size: Approximately 6
Total Cooking and Preparation Time: 2 hours and 45 minutes

Ingredients:

- ¾ cup of Ground Beef
- 2 Tbsp. Olive Oil
- 1 Large White Onion, Chopped
- 1 Garlic Clove, Crushed
- 2 Tbsp. of Worcestershire Sauce
- 1 Tbsp. Balsamic Vinegar
- 1 tsp. Oregano, Dried
- 2 Beef Bouillon Cubes

- 1 Can of Italian Tomatoes
- ½ Yellow and Red Pepper, de-seeded and sliced thinly
- 3 Large Carrots, peeled and Finely Chopped
- 1 Tbsp. of Tomato Puree
- 1 Can of Tomato Soup
- ¼ Cup of Red Wine
- 1 Bay Leaf
- Dash of Salt And Pepper To Taste

For The Topping

- 3 Large Potatoes, Quartered
- ¼ cup of Butter
- ¼ Milk or Heavy Cream
- ¼ Grated Parmesan Cheese

Directions:

1. The first thing that you will need to do is to first cook the meat you are going to use for this recipe. In a large saucepan add olive oil and heat until the oil is hot. Add the ground beef and sear on medium or high heat for 20 minutes or until meat is browned.

2. Next add your onions and cook for 10 minutes over low heat. Add your carrots, 1 bay leaf and crushed garlic for 3 minutes, stirring frequently.

3. Add the Worcestershire sauce, red wine and balsamic vinegar and cook over medium heat for about 4 minutes. Then add the rest of your ingredients and lower the heat until it reaches a nice simmer. Leave it to simmer for about an hour.

To Make The Topping:

1. Boil a few potatoes in a pot of boiling water and boil just until they are softened.

2. Drain out the boiling water and return to low heat. Mash the potatoes in a large bowl and add your butter and milk or cream. Mix until mixture is smooth.

3. Add a dash of salt and pepper to taste.

Finish It Off:

1. You will next need to spoon your meat mixture into a separate serving dish. Spoon your potatoes mixture over the top and crimp your dish using a fork. Sprinkle some grate cheese on the top and place into your Halogen oven. Cook at 420 degrees for about 30 minutes or until the dish is golden brown on top. Serve.

Delicious Mediterranean Cajun Fish

If you are looking for a healthy and delicious dish to make for your family tonight, this is definitely the recipe for you. With this recipe you can use practically any kind of fish that you love whether it is salmon, sea bass or even cod. With this recipe you will be able to cook your fish to perfection while still maintaining all of the essential vitamins and natural flavors that you are craving.

Serving Size: 1

Total Cooking and Preparation Time: Approximately 35 minutes

Ingredients:

- A piece of fish, both skinned and de-boned
- 1 Yellow Onion, Chopped
- ½ of a Red Pepper, Chopped and De-Seeded
- ½ tsp of Cajun Seasoning
- 2 Tbsp. Olive Oil
- Pinch of Salt and Pepper to Taste
- ¼ cup White Wine

- 10 Fresh Basil Leaves
- 6 Lettuce Leaves
- Zest of an Orange
- 1 Orange, Cut Into Segments
- 8 Black Olives, Deseeded and Chopped Into Halves
- 1 Sprig of Dill

Directions:

1. Wash your cut of fish thoroughly and leave to dry on a paper towel.

2. Season the fish with some Cajun seasoning, salt and pepper.

3. Wrap your fish in tin foil and add your white wine. Seal the tin foil and let your fish marinate for about 20 minutes.

4. Using a separate mixing bowl, add you basil leaves, lettuce leaves, orange, orange zest, black oils, 1 Tbsp. of Olive oil, some salt and pepper and your sprig of dill. Thoroughly mix.

5. Next place your marinated fish into your halogen oven and cook at 390 degrees for at least 15 minutes. Turn off the oven and let your fish stand for 3 minutes before removing it. Your fish should be opaque in color and flake slightly when you use a fork on it.

6. Rest your slightly cooled fish on top of the salad that you made and serve.

The Best Halogen Oven Cheeseburger

This dish is a favorite dinner recipe to make that is great to have during the Super Bowl or whenever you are watching your favorite sport. You have a variety of options available to you such as adding whatever ingredients you want to make your cheeseburger your very own. Kids can get in on the fun and help to make their own special burger and this recipe is sure to please even the pickiest children.

Serving Size: Approximately 6

Total Cooking and Preparation Time: About 1 Hour

Ingredients:

- ¼ cup of Bread Crumbs
- 1 Lb. of Ground Beef
- 1 Large Onion, Sliced Into Quarters
- 2 Cloves of Garlic, Skinned and Crushed
- 1 tsp. of Cumin Seeds
- 1 tsp. Mixed Herbs
- 2 Tbsp. of Worcestershire Sauce

- 1 Tbsp. Sweet Chili Sauce
- 1 Egg
- Dash of Salt and Pepper to Taste
- A Dash of Olive Oil

For The Topping:
- 12 Slices of Regular White Bread
- 6 Slices of Sharp Cheddar Cheese
- A few Leaves of Lettuce
- 2 Large Tomatoes, Thinly Sliced
- 1 Red Onion, Sliced Thinly
- A Drop or Two of Olive Oil
- Some Ketchup
- Salt and Pepper to Taste

Directions:

1. Add your breadcrumbs to the ground beef and thoroughly mix together until both are thoroughly combined. Once mixed divide the meat into small balls and flatten until they are 1 inch thick.

2. Once flattened brush your hamburger patties with a little olive oil on both sides and place into your halogen oven to bake at 350 degrees for 10 minutes or until they are golden brown. Turnover and cook for 8 minutes or until golden brown.

3. Place a slice of cheddar cheese onto each burger and allow for the cheese to melt.
4. As the cheese is melting brush both sides of your slices of brush with some olive oil and let them toast until they are a light golden brown on both sides. You will need to do this until every piece of bread is toasted to perfection.

5. Once your burgers and bread are done baking, you will begin to assemble your burger adding whatever condiments you want. To hold the burgers together I recommend skewer each burger with a toothpick and drizzle some olive oil on top to finish it off. Serve with some French fries and enjoy.

Ham and Cheese Toasted Sandwiches

This recipe is incredibly easy to make and makes for a quick and easy breakfast or a great tasting snack. You can add whatever fillings you want to make it your own or you can add classy ingredients to make it look fancy.

Serving Size: 4

Total Cooking and Preparation Time: Approximately 15 minutes

Ingredients:

- 8 slices of Whole Wheat or White Bread
- Butter, To Use To Spread Onto Bread
- 8 Slices of Sharp Cheddar Cheese
- 8 Slices of Honey Ham, Thinly Sliced
- 2 tsp. Mustard

Directions:

1. You need to assemble your sandwich first. After you have spread butter onto all of your slices of bread form

your sandwich however you want. Add mustard last before you add the finally slice of bread to complete your sandwich.

2. Place your sandwiches onto the highest cooking rack and cook your sandwiches in your halogen oven at 480 degrees or until golden brown on both sides. Serve with French fries or potato chips and enjoy.

Delicious Roasted Potatoes

If you have ever wanted to make the most delicious roasted potatoes that will go along with virtually any meat dish that you prepare, this is the perfect recipe for you. These potatoes are crispy both on the inside and the outside and go great with roast chicken or a side of roast beef.

Serving Size: 4

Total Cooking and Preparation Time: Approximately 55-65 minutes

Ingredients:

- 8 Red Potatoes, Washed and Cubed
- A Dash of Sea Salt To Taste
- 2 Tbsp. of Butter, Melted
- Dash of Black Pepper to Taste
- Fresh Thyme and Rosemary

Directions:

1. Cut your red potatoes after you wash them into cubes. Boil them in water for 5 minutes and then drain.

2. Place your potatoes into a roasting pan and season with salt, pepper and butter. Add your rosemary and thyme and toss until seasoned fully.

3. Roast in your halogen oven at 480 degree for 20 minutes. Then reduce the heat to 450 and cook for another 35-45 minutes. Last heat the oven back up to 480 degree and cook for an additional 20 minutes.

4. Remove from heat and allow to cool slightly before serving.

Great Tasting Desserts

Miniature Christmas Cupcakes

These perfect tiny cupcakes are great to bring out during a Christmas celebration with your family. They are incredibly easy to make and can be made using small muffin tins or silicon tins. If you prefer to make them beautiful to look at you can use muffin liners in the colors green and red. A little tip for you: if you on a gluten free or wheat free diet you can switch the kind of flour you use to wheat or gluten free flour.

This Recipe Makes: 10-15 Mini Cupcakes

Ingredients:

- ½ cup of Butter
- ½ cup of Sugar
- 2 Eggs
- ¼ cup of Cocoa, Sifted Beforehand
- 1/3 cup Flour, Sifted Beforehand
- 2-3 Tbsp. of Icing Sugar
- Water

- Colored Icing In The Colors Red and Green

Directions:

1. First beat the ½ cup of butter and the ½ cup of sugar together until the mixture is both light and fluffy.

2. Next add in the eggs and make sure that you beat it well.

3. Next add in your sifted cocoa and flour. You will need to fold these two ingredients in and fold until they are thoroughly combined.

4. Once fully mixed add the batter into your muffin tins.

5. Preheat your Halogen oven to 380 degrees Fahrenheit. Place your muffin tin on the lowest rack and cook for 8-12 minutes. To test if the muffins are done prick with a toothpick. If they are firm and springy, they are done.

6. Remove from your oven and place on a rack to cool.

7. Mix your icing sugar with a small amount of water and add it slowly at a time until it reaches a thick consistency.

8. As soon as the cupcakes are cool icing your cupcakes alternatively in red and green icing.

9. Leave alone for icing to set and serve in a few minutes time.

Bake well Pastries

This delicious pastry originated in England and is a dessert that consists of a short crust pastry filled with a layer of delicious jam. When you bake this you will undoubtedly impress your guests with your incredible baking abilities.

Serving Size: 6 to 8

Ingredients:

- Raspberry jam
- 1 X 20-22 cm Pre-baked Pastry Case
- 2/3 cup of Butter
- 2/3 cup of Sugar
- 1 Egg, Beaten
- ¼ cup of Flour
- 2/3 cup of Almonds, Ground
- ½ cup of Icing Sugar
- ¼-1/2 cup of Cold Water

Directions:

1. Place a thin layer of raspberry jam into your pastry case. Put this off to one side.

2. In a separate bowl beat both the sugar and butter together until the combination is both fluffy and light.

3. Next beat in your egg. Then add in the flour and ground almonds.

4. Once you are done mixing spoon your mixture over the jam and make sure that you spread it until it is even.

5. Preheat your Halogen oven to 350 degrees Fahrenheit. Once heated place your pastries onto the highest rack and cook for about 20-25 minutes or until the pastry itself is golden brown and it is cooked thoroughly.

6. Remove from your oven and set aside to cool.

7. As your pastries are cooling you will want to create your icing. Take the icing sugar and add a few drops of water at a time until the icing reaches the perfect consistency.

8. Once your pastries are fully cooled you will then add a thin layer of icing over it. Let the icing set and then serve with a cup of coffee or tea.

Sweet Bread and Butter Pudding

I know that once in a while you may find yourself having an extra croissant left over and that you don't know what to do with it. Well, this is a recipe that you can use to make something delicious with your left-overs.

Ingredients:

- 2 Croissants
- Dried Fruit (Choose whichever one you like. For instance I used raisins in this recipe).
- A half-pint of Milk
- 2 Tbsp. of Sugar
- 1 Egg

Directions:

1. Lightly grease a straight sided bowl or a small soufflé dish.

2. Slice your croissants thinly and set inside your bowl.

61

3. Sprinkle in a bit of the pieces of fruit into your slices.

4. Preheat your Halogen oven to 350 degrees Fahrenheit and set your bowl on the lowest rack.

5. In a separate bowl add your milk, sugar and egg. Whisk until completely blended. Pour this mixture over your croissant slices.

6. Add some more dried fruit on top of the slices and if you want sprinkle a touch of cinnamon onto each.

7. Place in your oven and cook for approximately 15 to 20 minutes or until the insides form a dome shape and are golden brown.

8. Remove from oven and set aside to cool. Serve with coffee, tea or a shot of rum and enjoy.

Classy Stained Glass Rounds

This recipe is one which you can use both to impress your guests and to use to add a little flair to your Christmas tree. You can even use this to give to your family and close friends as a special gift. These tasty treats are sure to bring out the little kid out of everybody and will surely surprise those who eat it.

Whenever you see a stained glass window, you cannot help but smile and admire its beauty. With this recipe you can create your own beautiful works of art and you can make them into something your entire family will admire.

This Recipe Makes: Approximately 24 Rounds

Ingredients:
- ½ cup of Butter
- ¼ cup of Sugar
- ¾ cup of Flour
- 1 Egg Yolk
- 24 Colored Sweets, Boiled

Directions:

1. Preheat your Halogen oven to 375 degrees Fahrenheit. As your oven heats up grease 3 large baking trays.

2. In a separate medium sized bowl and add the butter and sugar. Beat both until the consistency is both creamy and light.

3. Add the egg yolk and flour into your mixture and mix together until combined thoroughly.

4. Add batter onto a floured surface and using a rolling pin roll until it is approximately 1 centimeter thick.

5. With a cookie cutter cut out the shapes that you want and place the cookies onto your baking sheet. Then use a smaller cookie cutter in order to make the center of each cookie.

6. Take one boiled sweet and place it into the center of each cookie and bake in your oven for about 15-20 minutes until the cookies are a golden brown color and until the sweet middle is fully melted.

7. Remove from the oven and allow to cool completely on a separate baking sheet. Upon cooling, serve or wrap as a gift and enjoy.

Early Morning Fruit Scones

One of the most traditional dishes you can have on an early morning, these fruit scones are a perfect addition to any cup of coffee or tea. Great for guests and people of all ages these scones are great to have while you are bonding with your family or creating new memories with the people that you love.

Serving Size: Approximately 12

Total Cooking and Preparation Time: 30 minutes

Ingredients:

- ½ cup of All Purpose Flour
- A Dash of Salt
- 1 tsp. of Cream of Tartar
- ½ tsp of Baking Soda
- ¼ cup of Sugar
- 4 Tbsp. Butter
- 1/3 mixed fruit
- Half a Pint of Milk

Directions:

1. Preheat your halogen oven to 375 degrees and lightly grease a baking sheet.

2. In a mixing bowl combine the flour, cream of tartar, salt, baking soda, sugar and butter until thoroughly mixed.

3. Next add your mixed fruit and mix using a wooden spoon.

4. Next you will need to slowly add your milk until you have a firm dough.

5. On a lightly floured surface roll your dough until it is 1 inch in thickness. Cut out round pieces of dough using a round cookie cutter.

6. On a greased baking sheet place your dough rounds and make sure that you leave enough space between them to allow them to expand while they bake.

7. Brush the tops of your rounds with some milk and add onto the lowest rack of your oven. Bake the rounds for 15 minutes or until they are golden brown in color. Remove from the oven and place them on a rack to cool

8. Serve with jam, butter or cream cheese and your favorite cup of coffee and tea. Enjoy!

Banana and Carrot Cake

If you have been searching for the most delicious and most cake recipe, you don't have to look any further. This cake includes a perfect combination of both banana and carrot which helps to give this cake the right amount of sweetness and texture. This cake is great to make during the holidays or when you are having a sweet tooth.

Serving Size: 8

Total Cooking and Preparation Time: About 1 hour and 35 minutes

Ingredients:

- 2 Ripe Bananas, Sliced and Mashed
- ¾ cup of Sunflower Oil
- 1/3 cup of Dark Brown Sugar
- 4 Large Eggs, Beaten Lightly
- ¼ cup Carrots, Grated
- 1/4 cup of Sultanas
- ¼ cup Walnuts
- Zest 2 Medium Sized Oranges

- Juice From 1 Orange
- 1 tsp. Baking Soda
- ½ tsp. Baking Powder
- 1 tsp. Ground Cinnamon
- 1-2 cups Flour
- ½ cup Cream Cheese
- 1/3 cup Powdered Sugar
- Lemon Zest

Directions:

1. Lightly grease a cake pan with butter and line the bottom of the pan with a baking sheet. Set aside.

2. Place your mashed banana, eggs, sugar, sultanas, walnuts, carrots, juice and zest into a large mixing bowl and mix until thoroughly combined.

3. Next add the flour, baking soda, baking powder and cinnamon and mix until entire mixture is smooth.

4. Then pour your batter into your cake pan. Place your cake into your halogen oven and back for 35 minutes at 350 degrees.

5. After 35 minutes you will want to turn the temperature down to 320 degrees and continue baking for an additional 30 to 40 minutes until it is done. Use a butter knife to skewer the cake and if the knife comes out clean, your cake is done.

The Icing

1. Beat the powdered sugar, Cream cheese and lemon zest until completely mixed and pipe onto your cake. Serve with ice cream and enjoy.

Moist Chocolate Brownies

This recipe makes the best brownies you will ever taste. With the crispy outer later and the moist center these brownies taste as if they were plucked right out of heaven. You can make this as a serve alone dessert or add it to a bowl of delicious ice cream. Whatever you choose to do your friends and family will be begging for you to make more.

Serving Size: 10

Total Cooking and Preparation Time: About 50 minutes

Ingredients:

- ½ cup of Unsalted Butter
- 1/3 cup of Cocoa
- 1/3 cup of Walnuts, Chopped
- ½ cup of Sugar
- ¼ cup of Flour, Sifted

- 2 Medium Sized Eggs
- ¼ cup of Milk Chocolate, Grated

Directions:

1. Melt your butter in a medium sized saucepan. Use only 1/3 of the total butter. Once melted add the cocoa and stir constantly until well blended. Set aside.

2. Using the remaining butter cream it into the sugar until it turns a pale color and then add the eggs. Beat the eggs one at a time until thoroughly mixed. Next add in your flour and fold it gently/

3. Add your walnuts and your chocolate mixture and mix until thoroughly combined.

4. Place your brownie batter onto a baking sheet and bake in your halogen oven at 350 degrees for at least 25-30 minutes.

5.Once done remove the brownies from your oven and place them on a separate rack to cool for about 10 minutes. Once cooled slice into small squares. Sprinkle your grated chocolate over them and enjoy.

Decadent Chocolate Sponge Cake

If you are a career chocoholic than this is the perfect recipe for you. This recipe is the lightest version of a chocolate cake that you can make and is every chocoholics dream. If you really wish for this cake to come out as light and fluffy as possible, the key to making that happen is whisking it. The harder you whisk it, the fluffier it will turn out to be.

Serving Size: 8

Total Cooking and Preparation Time: Approximately 1 hour

Ingredients:

- ½ cup of Butter
- 4 Medium Sized Eggs
- ½ cup of Sugar
- ½ Cup of Flour, Sifted
- 1 tsp. of Baking Powder
- ¼ cup of Cocoa Powder
- 1 Cup of Dark Chocolate, Melted
- 2 cups Heavy Cream

- 2 tsp. Of Vanilla Extract
- 4 Tbsp. Of Jam

Directions:

1. Preheat your halogen oven to 350 degrees.

2. Cream your butter and sugar together with a whisk and do so until the mixture is both pale and fluffy.

3. Beat your eggs for at least 5 minutes until they turn very light in color and then slowly add your melted chocolate into the mixture.

4. Add your cocoa powder, baking powder and flour into your wet mixture and fold it very gently until they are thoroughly mixed together.

5. Add your batter into a greased cake pan and cook on the lowest rack of your halogen oven for 40 minutes or until the cake is springs back whenever you apply some pressure.

6. Remove your cake from the oven and set on a rack to cool for at least 10 minutes.

7. Once your cake cools add you heavy cream and vanilla extract together and thoroughly mix together. Place jam on top of your cake and pour cream and vanilla mixture over the top of it. Serve with ice cream and enjoy.

Conclusion

Using your Halogen oven is one of the best investments you have ever made. There are a variety of health benefits as well as cooking benefits to using your oven, but the best benefit of all is the fact that you are now able to make the most delicious recipes that will surely impress your guests and family.

Ever since the Halogen oven came out on the market in the United States, it has grown in popularity over the past couple of years and still continues to grow in popularity to this very day. Besides the fact that a Halogen oven is one of the best cooking tools that cooks food more efficiently than any conventional oven, it is also a healthier alternative to cooking one's food.

As long as you know what recipes to make and how to properly care for your Halogen oven, there is no doubt in my mind that you will be using your oven to make delicious food for your family and friends for many years to come.

Printed in Great Britain
by Amazon

49728183R00041